Sayed Abdullah Walizai

Improving Computer Education at Afghan Schools

AF190957

Sayed Abdullah Walizai

Improving Computer
Education at Afghan Schools

Study of Computer Education in developing
countries In context of Afghanistan

LAP LAMBERT Academic Publishing

Imprint

Any brand names and product names mentioned in this book are subject to trademark, brand or patent protection and are trademarks or registered trademarks of their respective holders. The use of brand names, product names, common names, trade names, product descriptions etc. even without a particular marking in this work is in no way to be construed to mean that such names may be regarded as unrestricted in respect of trademark and brand protection legislation and could thus be used by anyone.

Cover image: www.ingimage.com

Publisher:
LAP LAMBERT Academic Publishing
is a trademark of
Dodo Books Indian Ocean Ltd. and OmniScriptum S.R.L publishing group

120 High Road, East Finchley, London, N2 9ED, United Kingdom
Str. Armeneasca 28/1, office 1, Chisinau MD-2012, Republic of Moldova, Europe
Managing Directors: Ieva Konstantinova, Victoria Ursu
info@omniscriptum.com

Printed at: see last page
ISBN: 978-3-659-44711-2

Zugl. / Approved by: Berlin, Technical University of Berlin, 2013

Abstract

In our thesis the current computer education in Afghan schools is studied. We tried to analyze the current situation and based on finding we studied and researched for appropriate solutions. The computer educations in Afghan schools are facing several challenges. In order to improve computer education, the contents of this thesis are discussed on three important factors, which are computer syllabi, teacher proficiency and infrastructure. These three factors build up computer education curriculum for schools. Computer education in school is an important subject which needs broader attention of the policy-makers in the government to improve this subject. Computer education can help students for creative and abstract thinking and computer technology is almost used in every part of our daily life, hence students in schools must learn this field.

Table of Contents

Table of Figures

First Chapter

1.1 Introduction

Computers play a vital role in our daily life. We are engaged with computer and IT in our life; we use the benefits of them either directly or indirectly. However, computer and information technology is deployed in different sector of our life, but still majority of the people don't know what computer science is or the machinery or technology they are using how they work. The concept of Computer Science is always misunderstood among non-professional debates. The explicit difference between computer science and computer usage can't be recognized by public. The discussed problem is a global discussing issue, in our country Afghanistan, it is furthermore problematic. The IT is a new field and public are only aware of its usage, they can't think the idea behind the production of these technology. Therefore a broader attention for improving this sector is required.

In Afghanistan variety of different institutions are providing higher educations in IT. However, many people are interested to continue their studies in this filed but still majority of these interested beside non-interested students don't know what computer science or IT is. Moreover, computer science in school gives the opportunity to students to think logically and find solution to different problems. Therefore we found this necessary to improve computer education in Afghan schools. Although computer education is integrated in school studies, our work is to present constructive ideas to improve computer education at school.

In order to have viable approaches for improving computer education, we conducted a survey in different school across Afghanistan. We analyzed the current situation of Computer Education in schools through our survey. We worked based on our findings from our survey. In the scope of our master thesis we covered scientific approaches and solutions to the problems that are outlined in our finding.

The discussing issues of computer science and computer usage or IT gave us the idea to select the name of our work as "Improving Computer Education in Afghan Schools". In our work we will focus on ideas to cover both computer science and computer usage as computer education studies in schools.

The thesis is divided into five chapters. The first chapter presents the overall introduction to the thesis, followed by general overview to Afghanistan and terminologies. The second chapter presents information about Computer Science studies in Afghanistan. The results and analysis of our survey is presented in second chapter under the title of current Computer Education situation in schools. The third chapter focuses on how to improve the computer education syllabi in the school. The experience and scientific approaches used in other developed or developing countries for writing syllabi is reflected in this chapter. The fourth chapter explains the solution for teacher proficiency issues. The fifth chapter covers the suggestion and recommendation for developing infrastructure of computer education. Finally the last section is the conclusion of our work. In this part we will present our specific and concrete recommendation for the policy makers of education system in Afghanistan.

1.2 General Overview

1.2.1 Afghanistan

Afghanistan is a mountainous country located in the central Asia, which has border with Pakistan, Iran, Turkmenistan, Tajikistan, Uzbekistan and a narrow way in the high mountain to China. [1] Due to its important and strategic location, in history it is always the field of battles. Afghanistan got independence from British Empire in 1919, when Amanullah Khan was the king.

The current situation of the country is directly affected by the last four decades war. The four decades of war was started by revolution of communist group, followed by occupation of Soviet Union. After withdrawal of Soviet Union militaries, the war leads to civil war among different Afghan ethnic, religious and political groups. During the civil war the infrastructure and all bases for the newly developed country were destroyed. [2] However, still security threats exist, but after occupation of US-NATO troops to Afghanistan, the Afghans got the chance for developing their country.

Figure 1 Regional Map of Afghanistan.

Afghanistan is the house for different tribes, speaking with more than 30 languages. According to constitutional law which was written and approved by a grant assembly in 2002 among all languages; Pashto and Dari are official languages. [3] Majority of people are followers of different parties of Islam.

a. Security

The current security situation in Afghanistan is almost hopeless for broad development across all the country. Although, during the last decade many efforts were done by Afghan government with support of International Community to strengthen security situation; but still security risks prevents deployment of various projects. [2] The majority parts of the urban areas are controlled by the armed opposition of the government. The security risks arise from conflict of governmental forces against armed opposition. The security situation gets worsening. [4] This for sure affects all other sectors of the country.

3

b. Education

The education system in Afghanistan is highly affected from war of last four decades. In most parts of the country school buildings were destroyed during civil war and girls' educational facilities were restricted. [5] However, with intervention of international community the education system has fundamentally changed, but still a big number of children don't have access to education facilities. Due to high risk of security standard education is not deployed in all over Afghanistan. The education sector grew dramatically in both quantity and quality. There are around 5 million students who need to go to school but don't have access to it, however 10 million students are involved in education system. Although education system is in the process of developing, but still it have variety of problems such as: infrastructure, teacher proficiency, and standard curriculum, security threats for students, teachers and physical facilities.

According to reports around 63 percent of teachers are not qualified to teach in schools. Around 43 percent of all schools don't have proper classrooms and only 129 vocational schools in Afghanistan are operating. [5] In the south and south west of country security threats caused several schools to be closed.

The standard curriculums rewriting for school is started in 2002 and up to now hundreds of books are written, compiled and published for different levels of schools. The new curriculums still have some problems which will be reviewed after each period of four years. [6] The published books are distributed to major cities; however students in urban areas still don't have complete access to these books.

c. Infrastructure

The infrastructure in Afghanistan was destroyed. The cities connecting roads, agriculture, watering system, power energy, telecommunication, economy, campus buildings and other sectors were in some cases completely destroyed and some cases they were badly affected. [7] The international community in last decade had remarkable attention to infrastructure. In result growth in this era is a great achievement of Afghanistan government.

4

Power energy or electricity is always the challenging part when discussing about infrastructure. The Afghan government bought electricity from neighboring countries, while they didn't invest on internal resources. Afghanistan has the facilities for producing water, solar and wind electricity. [8] The bought electricity from neighboring countries is not enough for all parts of Afghanistan, therefore education system and technology is facing with the lack of energy in most of the cases. This indeed effects on quality education specifically IT education in schools.

d. Information Technology

Modern telecommunications technology was started in Afghanistan by a small exchange build in Kabul in 1930. Due to conflict and civil war infrastructures were destroyed. In the process of different sectors reconstruction and rehabilitation in Afghanistan, Internet services are also one of the sectors started developing since 2002. New and first ICT policy by government was adopted in October 2002. Different project are running in this sector to achieve best performance. [9]

The Internet was recognized as an important source for changing the current situation in the country in 2002. In 2003 a domain name ".af" was given legally to Afghanistan, and the Afghanistan Network Information Center (AFGNIC) was established to manage domain names. All telecommunications, operations and services were transferred into a newly created national telecommunications carrier company called "Afghan Telecom", through a presidential decree [10].

Today Afghanistan supports many hosts and seven main Internet Services Providers (ISPs), a growing number of Internet cafés and mobile communication private companies (GSM). A big project is running to connect the country (and neighboring nations) along major highways through Afghan Telecom's "National Optical Fiber" backbone project. In the past decade (2002-till now) broad and significant deployment of IT and its services all around Afghanistan is a great achievement of the government and international society.

e. Software localization needs and status

However, majority of Afghanistan's citizen are illiterate, literates are also only able to deal with local languages. Therefore the usage of new technology in such environment is directly affected, because new technologies are mostly present with international languages interface. There are too many problems with Afghanistan's local languages which are Arabic scripted with adoption to new technologies.

However, the Ministry of Information and Communication Technology hired a commission to work on localization of major Software (e.g. Windows, Office, and Linux) into Afghan (Pashto and Dari) languages, but commission was dismissed after completion of a specific version of the mentioned products. The Ministry of Education proposed to localize the XO (One laptop per child) to Pashto and Dari. They succeeded in the mission and localized the operating system along with some other literacy game and applications. [11] Although individual efforts in this area should be mentioned but overall all efforts are negligible.

1.2.2 What is Curriculum?

The term "Curriculum" had various concepts during the past history. The historical questions that were conceptualized from curriculum were: How long it is? What kind of things does it contain? What things it should contain? What is the best way to organize these contents? How should things be taught? What contents are for? What should children learn, in what sequence, and by what methods? [12] Answer to all mentioned question which were evolved during the past history were discussed and developed under curriculum concept.

There are different definitions for the term curriculum which are defined by different scholars. For better understanding of the concept, we will present some definition to this term. It is to mention that these definitions are outlined in "Selected Concepts of Curriculum" [13]:

1. "A sequence of potential experiences is set up in the school for the purpose of disciplining children and youth in group ways of thinking and acting. This set of experiences is referred to as the curriculum." (Smith, et al., 1957)

2. "A general over-all plan of the content or specific materials of instruction that the school should offer the student by way of qualifying him for graduation or certification or for entrance into a professional or vocational field." (Good, 1959)

3. "A curriculum is a plan for learning." (Taba, 1962)

4. "All the experiences a learner has under the guidance of the school." (Foshay, 1969)

5. "The planned and guided learning experiences and intended outcomes, formulated through the systematic reconstruction of knowledge and experience, under the auspices of the school, for the learner's continuous and willful growth in person-social competence." (Tanner and Tanner, 1975)

6. "Curriculum is often taken to mean a course of study. When we set our imaginations free from the narrow notion that a course of study is a series of textbooks or specific outline of topics to be covered and objectives to be attained, broader more meaningful notions emerge. A curriculum can become one's life course of action. It can mean the paths we have followed and the paths we intend to follow. In this broad sense, curriculum can be viewed as a person's life experience." (Connelly and Clandinin, 1988)

7. "Curriculum is a cultural reproduction in a structured way. It is even more: It should also value independent thinking in the context of the widest sense of social responsibility. (Smith, Stanley & Shores)

In short words we can say curriculum is a dynamic, ever-changing series of planned learning experiences or curriculum is everything learners experience in school. To conclude the discussion regarding curriculum we can say curriculum include all aspects for the teaching process, including teaching content, teaching aims, teaching materials, teaching methodology and teaching disciplines which will differ according to necessity of each society. In our context we will divide the curriculum improving concept into discussion about syllabi, infrastructure and teacher proficiency.

1.2.3 What are syllabi?

As discussed earlier our aim is to improve IT education in Afghan schools, which will focus on curriculum. There is a doubt regarding curriculum and syllabi. Therefore it is necessary to have definition about this term too. The term syllabi are defined as follow:

"A general overall plan of the content that the school should offer the student by way of qualifying him for graduation or certification or for entrance into a professional or vocational field." (Good,1973:149)

This means that syllabi are the list of content which an institution will cover in a specific period of time for certification or promoting from one grade to another. As part of our work we will also focus on current IT syllabi of Afghan schools and then we will present our suggestion for improving them.

1.2.4 What is Information Technology (IT)?

Information Technology is a field which focuses on processing of information by a computer. This means that information is managed and delivers by combination of hardware, software, services and infrastructure. IT helps to produce, manipulate, store, communicate, and/or disseminate information. Our daily life is evolving with advent of new technology. There are thousands of examples from the usage of IT in our daily life (e.g. cell phones, ecommerce services, ATM machines).

IT was and is game changer in other sectors, the same IT can change the education system. The broad achievement in our daily life is the impacts of IT. IT with enabling new models can help higher education to serve new groups of students, in greater numbers, and with better learning outcomes. Due to revolution of IT, currently millions of books are available online (e.g., Google Books); lectures come in all formats (e.g., podcasts, YouTube, Khan Academy). IT brought the opportunity for academic exchange services besides delivering information (e.g.Smartthinking) and online courses (e.g. StraighterLine). Students, lecturers, administrators and employee can have access to colleges or universities for student services, instruction, or library anytime and anywhere. [14]

Second Chapter

2.1 Computer education in Afghanistan

Computer Science studies are officially started in Kabul University in 1995 by forming Computer Science department in Science Faculty. [15] Beside this official institution that was offering bachelor degree in Computer Science, there were few other private courses that were providing application's usage training on that time. IT education facilities were growing up slowly. After the new government in 2002, these facilities grew up dramatically. The government adopted some policies through which computer education facilities were established all over Afghanistan. Although there were different governmental universities that were offering computer science education, too many private institutions also start operating. The IT education was available in major cities and variety of interested people had access to them. IT education is available now in different field for different purposes. Governmental institutions are offering two year diploma and bachelor degree, while private institutions are offering different certification. They are providing from short term trainings to Master degree.

All of these facilities were for higher education. On the school level, some private courses were offering application's usage training. Ministry of Education had a project to deliver computer education in a cheaper way to the students, so they implemented the "One-laptop-per-Child" project. This project covered some schools and they distribute some cheap computer and held trainings for the students. [11] Due to lack of funding in this project, it was stopped and only few schools were covered by this project.

It is to mention that some other non-governmental organizations were offering Computer application's training in some schools. Some organization is funding schools to setup computer facilities and some others are directly implementing computer education in schools. ISAF (PRT teams), Asia Foundation, GTZ, USAID are funding schools and Help the Afghan Children organization have classes in schools that are offering Computer Education. [16]

9

2.1.1 Institutions

In 2009, Kabul University, Kabul Polytechnic University, Kabul Education University, Nangarhar University, Herat University, Khost University and six private universities were offering bachelor degree in Computer Science. [15] Nowadays, beside the above mentioned governmental universities Konar University, Balkh University and more than 50 private universities are offering bachelor degree in Computer Science. One governmental institute is offering bachelor in Telecommunication and three other governmental institutions are offering two year diploma in Computer Science and Engineering. Two Kabul based private universities are offering Master degree in Computer Science. There are more than hundred private courses that are offering short term training of Computer Science and Computer applications.

2.1.2 Curriculum

In 1995 the first official Computer Science Department was established in Kabul University. The curriculum for this department was copied from some private University from Peshawar of Pakistan and it was adopted by a non-governmental organization. In 2002 the new administration made changes to it. They found the opportunity to learn from experience of other countries. In 2002 the Cisco Academy build their local Academies in Kabul, Kabul Education, Khost, Herat and Balkh University. They offered their own curriculum and it was part of computer science department lectures. In 2004 Computer Science Faculty was established in Herat University with support of TU-Berlin. This faculty was functioning based on the curriculum which was developed in TU-Berlin. [15]

Other governmental universities also updated their curriculum according to the need of society and international standard. Private universities had different curriculum then governmental, they had the most updated syllabi and were taught by high qualified lectures.

The school syllabi for Computer Education were developed in late 2011. These syllabi are written for high school. [6] But still the Ministry of Education is lacking the standard curriculum for Computer Education. They only wrote the syllabus and provide some infrastructure in few schools.

2.1.3 Infrastructure

The IT is a newly established field and there were no infrastructure available for this sector before the civil war. Therefore, in 2002 the initial infrastructure forming was started in this area. However, in IT education sector, infrastructure was and is poor, but it is evolving day by day. Some governmental efforts in this section are mentionable and some international organization tried their best to provide infrastructure in IT education institutions. A team from Technical University of Berlin formed several IT infrastructure facilities in different universities of Afghanistan. [15] The Cisco Academy built Computer Labs in few universities. Still the overall problem of infrastructure exist which affect IT education. Some of universities don't have proper buildings, electricity, Internet connection and other necessary hardware.

In the schools infrastructure for providing computer education is too poor. Only few schools have functioning Computer Labs. Majority of schools don't have access to Internet and electricity. [17]

2.1.4 Human Resources (Capacity Building)

The IT education facilities were lacking with high qualified and expert lecturers in their start. As Computer Science was a newly established department in Kabul University, therefore few of the lecturers were qualified. Capacity building process of the lecturers was started by offering online Master program in Computer Science by USAID. [15]

The Technical University of Berlin also offered several scholarships for Master in Computer Science. The 24 Master graduates from mentioned university are currently backed to their universities and are serving as lecturers. [18] Currently 24 lecturers from different universities are doing their Master in TU-Berlin and it is planned that 25 others will also join the Master in 2013. The same other organizations also offered different capacity building programs which helped the institutions to gain experience and provide standard education.

As mentioned in above section, private universities offered classes with lecturers that are qualified and expert. They hired lecturers from Pakistan, India and other countries. For sure in some cases private universities have worse output then governmental.

The situation of IT education in schools is very different. There are few teachers in some schools that studied Computer Science. Majority of the teachers are not able to use computer. They are not professionals and only teach computer education as theory. [19]

The Kabul Education University is the only institution that is training Computer teachers for schools. Computer Science department in this university is graduating average 60 students yearly. [20] However, this number is quite low due to the demand of the professional computer teachers in the school, but majority of these graduates also don't join duty as computer teacher in the school.

2.2 Current situation of Computer Education in schools

Computer Education in Afghan school is officially running now. In the curriculum guide for Ministry of Education it is mentioned that all governmental and non-governmental school should have computer education as subject for 10th, 11th and 12th grade. [21] This curriculum guide is published in 2011 and before that all efforts for IT education were not officially recognized by the Ministry of Education in Afghanistan. In 2003 a non-governmental organization "Help the Afghan Children" implemented some projects, through which they develop computer labs in some governmental schools. They hired computer teachers for these schools and held computer education trainings. [16]

Some other organizations also held Computer Education training for school's students and some funding agencies built Computer Labs in some schools. However, there is little attention in this sector but still officials in Ministry of Education and schools administrators don't know the importance of computer education in schools. Hence, further development in this area is affected.

Schools in major cities of Afghanistan face the lack of qualified teachers, IT infrastructure and a standard syllabus. This situation is too bad in other low level provinces and urban areas. Majority of schools don't have proper building for delivering courses to the students. For recognizing these all problems, analyzing them and providing specific suggestions for improvement in computer education, we conduct several surveys. We explain our finding in this section.

2.2.1 Our work

IT play vital role in our daily life. Therefore a broader attention for improving this sector is required. As mentioned in previous sections, a variety of different institutions are providing higher education in computer science. However, many people are interested to continue their studies in this filed but still majority of these interested beside non-interested students don't know what computer science or IT is. Therefore we thought the better approach to solve this confusion is to integrate computer education in school. Although computer education is integrated in school studies our aim is to improve computer education in school. For improving computer education in Afghan schools, it is necessary to analyze and review the current situation. Afterward based on the findings we propose our plan for strengthening and improving computer education.

We conducted several surveys, gathered ideas from different categories of computer education supplier, did school visits, collect computer education syllabi and met some authorities in Ministry of Education.

Schools were the first and main sources which provided us the information about Computer Education. We conduct two surveys to gather information from schools. One survey was to collect data about overall situation of schools and infrastructure. The target of this survey was the administration of schools. We distributed 33 questioners for different school administrators in Kabul, Nangarhar, Kandahar, Herat and Balkh provinces. It was required to get permission from the Ministry of Education to contact school

13

administration; therefore the school selection for this survey was done by the authorities in the Ministry of Education offices. All the questioners are then merged and analyzed in spreadsheets and a summary of this survey is provided in Appendix I.

The second survey was to collect idea of teachers whom are teaching computer education in schools. They provided us information about their students, teaching skills and facilities, computer education syllabi and more. We distributed 48 questioners in above mentioned 33 schools. All the questionnaires are then merged and analyzed in spreadsheet and a quantitative summary of this survey is provided in Appendix II and a summary of teachers' ideas which were written in the questioner is provided in Appendix III.

The second key source was the officials in Ministry of Education who were involved in IT education process. We sent several questioners to these officials in Ministry of Education but, only received back 3 of these questioners. A summary of their ideas and experiences is provided in Appendix IV.

Our next target group was computer science professionals whom are involved in computer education in higher education institute. We thought these computer science professionals will give us constructive ideas for improving computer education based on necessities of Afghan society and computer science higher education institutions requirements. We sent questioners to some of these lecturers in Kabul, Kabul Poly Technic, Nangarhar, Herat and Kabul Education Universities. We received back only 9 questioners and a summary of their ideas for improving computer education is provided in Appendix V.

Besides conducting the above surveys we had visits from school in Kabul. The surveys in provinces were conducted by phone rather than directly visiting school's administrators and teachers. We collect different books and other publication regarding computer education and curriculum from Ministry of Education and interviewed some other influence authorities. Here, afterward we present our finding under different subtitles.

2.2.2 School syllabi for computer education

The current syllabi for computer education in Afghan schools is written and published in 2011 (1390). These syllabi are written for three grade of high school (10th, 11th and 12th grade). They are published in high quality and written in Pashto and Dari language. Majority of School administrators in Kabul and provinces claim that yet we didn't receive complete book that fulfill our needs. [17] These syllabi are written by two professional computer scientists and then they are approved and finalized by Education Curriculum Committee of Ministry of Education. [22] [23] [24]

The syllabi have too many problem, but teachers whom were involved in teaching process they have different opinions regarding these contents. Some are thinking these content are well and based on the need of our society and some other reject and says these syllabi should be written by a professional committee rather than individual writers. It is to mention that the majority of teachers in schools were not professional and their ideas about syllabi are also not from professional perspective. Here is the summary of teachers' idea regarding these syllabi [19]:

- This curriculum is better and will help the students for their daily activities.
- The level of current curriculum is higher than the literacy level of the students, while it focuses more on practical concepts but there is no facility available in most of the schools for practical work.
- The application which are reflected in the curriculum are out dated, the curriculum should reflect the latest version of the applications.
- The syllabus written for 10 and 11 grades are not well sorted, we recommend a step by step presenting of the concepts. The syllabus which are developed in current curriculum don't contain well aspects, it should have aspects which are needed for the students daily life. It would be better to have each application for the whole grade instead to split it into several grades.
- Schools don't receive the books of curriculum on time so the students can't get the entire content well.

- The syllabus on current curriculum is well designed and the contents are based on the knowledge level of the students but there are no professional teachers to teach them.
- The curriculum should be reviewed and approved by professional experts of Computer Science. It should be reviewed in consideration to the needs and opportunities of Afghan society.
- The first parts of the books reflect Internet usage; it would be nice to have theoretical concepts instead. Most of the parts in the syllabus are repeated, therefore for each grade separate syllabus should be written.

We received the digital copy of these syllabi and here after we present our finding from reviewing these concepts. The first book for 10th grade is started by overall information about Computer machine and its types and usage. Afterward the discussion about hardware and software is presented. Major parts in the beginning focus on computer hardware devices. Information regarding computer security is also reflected. In software section operating systems and application software are discussed. Thick part of the book describes the usage of Windows XP and its application. The last chapter focuses on computer networks and Internet. [24]

The second book for 11th grade is started by long discussion about computer usage in daily life. It is followed by the repeated section of hardware introduction. Afterward, health concern regarding computer usage is discussed. Further usage of Windows XP is presented in a chapter and it is followed by the usage of Microsoft Word. Some parts of Microsoft PowerPoint are presented in a separate chapter. Book is closed by discussion about surfing Internet. [22]

The final or third book for grade 12th is started by a repeated section of computer usage in daily life. Computer Security is presented and remaining parts of Windows XP's usage is discussed. Microsoft PowerPoint and Microsoft Excel usage is the heavy section of this book. The last three chapters focus on computer and Internet networks. Most of these contents are repeated with broader concepts. [23]

To conclude this section we can say that the current syllabi focus more on computer usage then computer science. Even there is no discussion about what computer science is. It more presents facts and usage of applications then theoretical concepts. Most of the parts are unnecessary repeated and there is no relation with each other. Although there are discussion about computer security but online security is not mentioned, which is an important aspect for teenagers. The main targets of the syllabi are to show students how to use Microsoft applications, in the meanwhile there is no discussion about property of this software. However, software types are discussed based on their usage, but different types of software like Open Source and Closed Source are not discussed. Overall as start point for writing syllabi, it can be count a good achievement. We describe our plan for improving them in later sections.

2.2.3 Infrastructures

Infrastructure is an important aspect to consider in computer education curriculum. As computer education is newly established subject in Afghan schools, therefore the required infrastructure is poor. There are some donating agencies which funded to develop and provide computer labs and other necessary hardware for computer education, but majority of schools are facing with the lack of necessary physical opportunities. In our visits from schools, we bullet-pointed some physical facilities as necessary aspect for delivering standard computer education. We cover 33 schools in our survey and the result regarding the infrastructure status is shown in "Figure 2 Infrastructure in Schools". However this data represent our survey, but it can't represent the actual situation of schools' infrastructure all over Afghanistan.

The actual situation for IT education in all schools of Afghanistan is too poor then founded in our survey. Too many schools in major cities and urban areas don't have proper buildings. There are even no or few computer machines for administrative activities in most of the schools. The amount of available computer labs or other physical facilities don't represent their active or running state. [17] Internet connection in some schools is only used by administration; it is not for educational purpose.

17

However, the Figure 2 Infrastructure in Schools state positive status of computer labs and library but these only reflect the availability. Overall the question about Computer library is replied as general library, but in fact the mention number is not correct about Computer library only few schools have a few number of books related to computer education. The same for Computer Labs, only few schools have well equipped and running Computer Labs, while other schools have Computer Labs with few inactive computer machines. There is only one projector in schools which are listed, that they have projector. There is no Internet connection for study purpose, what is stated in the figure show the availability of poor Internet for administration.

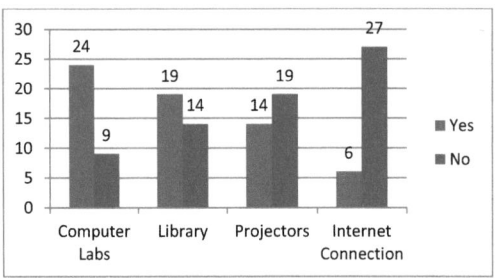

Figure 2 Infrastructure in Schools

Beside computer facilities power energy is another aspect which is part of infrastructure. Most of the schools in provinces and urban areas don't have power connection. Or in other words most of the schools in province and urban areas are not connected to electricity. The "Figure 3 Power Sources in Schools" shows the available power sources in our surveyed schools. Governmental power doesn't exist in all schools in province and urban areas. In few of the schools there are solar energy panels which are used to power up computer machines and some other schools used power generators. Administrators in schools that are equipped with power generators complain about the lack of budget for fueling the generators.

Most of the teachers are complaining from the physical facilities in their schools. They claim that the current syllabi are not practical due to lack of necessary infrastructure. The time which is allocated for a class to get computer lecture is too less due to lack of

18

available class rooms. The teachers say they are not able to deliver their lecture in 01:45 which is separated into three appointments of 00:35 minutes per week. [19] Overall necessary infrastructure which is the main part of implementing a curriculum doesn't exist in Afghan schools.

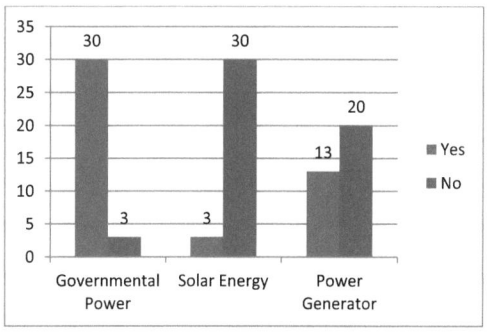

Figure 3 Power Sources in Schools

2.2.4 Teacher proficiency

The lack of professional teachers in Ministry of Education is an overall challenge. Computer Science is newly established field and there are few professionals in this field which have broader market. Students whom are studying the teacher training institution to be work as computer education teachers, after graduation; they prefers to work in other field rather than to be teachers in schools. Therefore, Afghan schools are facing the lack of professional teachers in computer education. There is a regulation approved by official authorities that students who are graduated from teacher training institution will not be hired in other sectors of government. However, government tries to hire professional teachers to schools based on this regulation, but still a broader market of non-governmental agencies is open for these graduates. In our survey from 33 schools 48 teachers had participated and they replied to our questions. Majority of the participants are non-professional and don't have basic knowledge about computer science. Although, some teachers obtained degrees in other fields; but they are currently teaching IT education. The "Figure 4 Teacher's Educational Level" shows the degree of our surveyed participants.

However, this figure indicates that, majority of the participants obtained bachelor degree; but these teachers obtained bachelor degrees in other fields; like English literature or mathematics only few of them are professional computer education teachers. The "Figure 5 Teachers' Proficiency Rate" shows the proficiency rate of the participated teachers in our survey.

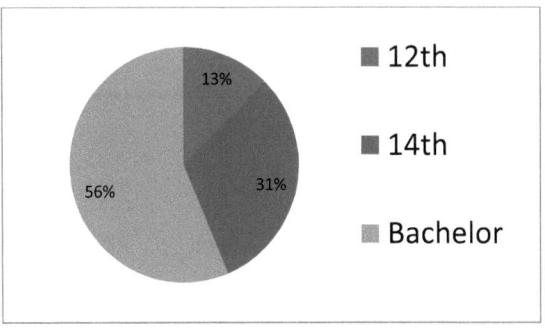

Figure 4 Teacher's Educational Level

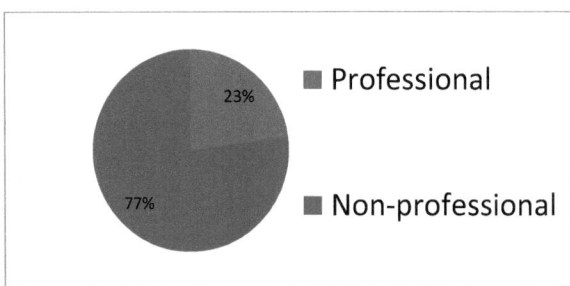

Figure 5 Teachers' Proficiency Rate

Majority of the teachers whom are currently teaching IT education in schools don't have basic knowledge of Computer Science. They only knew few application usage and they teach these application theoretically through white boards. [19] The "Figure 6 Teachers' Familiarity with Open Source" highlights the familiarity rate of teachers to Open Source community.

20

The facts taken from the above findings show that; there are few professional teachers whom are teaching IT education. Therefore there is a great demand to train and build the capacity of current teachers whom are involved in teaching process and train further teachers to fulfill the demand of schools.

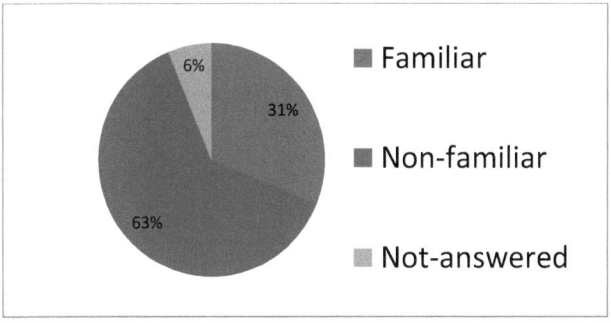

Figure 6 Teachers' Familiarity with Open Source

2.2.5 Security impacts

The Afghan people are suffering from security threats in different sides of their life. Computer education is also greatly affected by security threats. In most of the provinces and urban areas schools don't receive the desired support from governmental authorities due to the security concern. There are negligible infrastructures, no enough books to fulfill the needs and teachers are not receiving their salary on time. These indeed affect overall education, specifically computer education which require expensive infrastructure. Non-governmental organization also can't cover these areas for developing computer facilities on their schools.

2.2.6 Gender sensitivity

However, most of females in urban areas are prohibited to go to school, but computer education is treated equally in both cities and urban areas. The main reason would be that computer education is now a part of school's subjects and there is no restriction on it. In

21

other words those students whom are going to school either from male or female and are in high school receives computer education. In "Figure 7 Students' Gender" the number of students based on their gender whom are involved in computer education is shown. These numbers are from schools which were surveyed by us.

We found that in cities most of the schools have female teachers for providing computer education. The "Figure 8 Teachers' Gender" shows the number of teachers based on gender in our surveyed schools. The numbers of female teacher are more than the number of male teachers. These numbers represent the number of the computer education teachers in our surveyed schools.

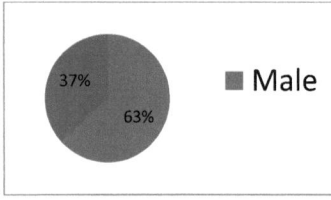

Figure 7 Students' Gender

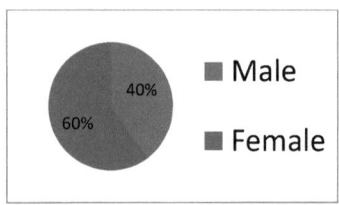

Figure 8 Teachers' Gender

2.2.7 Overview

As discussed in this part, there are many problems in IT education of Afghan schools. The poor infrastructure, lack of professional teachers and non-standard syllabi are the specification of current computer education in Afghan schools. In this part we reflect the idea of teachers whom are teaching computer education in schools.

In "Figure 9 Teacher's happiness rate from computer education" the reply of teachers' happiness from their teaching is expressed. This means majority of teachers along with too many problems are happy with computer education. The results in below figure reflect the ideas of teachers regarding overall computer education. However the question was originally asked to find idea of teachers regarding computer education status, but they replied to this question that they are happy with starting computer education in their school. The reason can be the interest of students and teacher to this vital field.

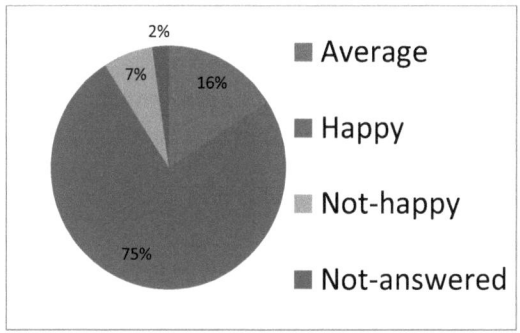

Figure 9 Teacher's happiness rate from computer education

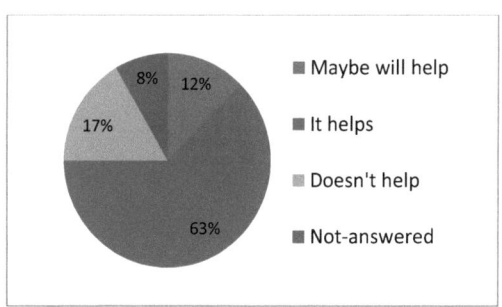

Figure 10 Future chances of students with current computer education

In reply of the question "How is the future chances of students with current Computer Education Process?" majority of the teachers replied that computer education will help the student for their future. Means their students will be able to get jobs or continue further in

23

the field of IT, if they study computer education in school. This reply indeed is not asked in the question the question specifically asks about the courses and lectures that these teachers are delivering to the students. Therefore the positive outcomes describe a different reply to the question. The result is shown in the figure below:

However, there are few facilities for delivering standard computer education, but still majority of the teachers claim that their lessons are good for the students. They say average of students can pass the examination quit well. The "Figure 11 Student passing rate in computer education courses" presents the passing rate of students in IT education in schools. As most of the lectures are delivered theoretically, so students learn it from books and therefore they are passing with good grades in theoretical concepts. In the real this result doesn't apply. Because the students don't learn what is planned in the curriculum they just learn whatever is in the book by reading from the book and remembering them theoretically. We were welling to include student's ideas in our survey too, but they were in winter vacation while our visit.

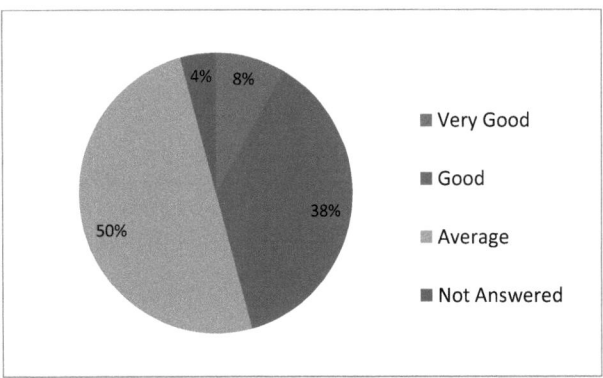

Figure 11 Student passing rate in computer education courses

Third Chapter

The third chapter presents scientific solutions and constructive suggestions for improvement of syllabi of computer education at schools. The scope of third chapter is divided into different subtitles, each section reflecting ideas, experience of other developed and developing countries and solution to computer education syllabi.

3.1 Improving computer education syllabi in schools

Computer education syllabi in Afghan schools are newly written and developed. As discussed in previous chapter, these syllabi are poor and need for renovation and improving. To deliver standard and efficient computer education, well written and on international standard syllabi are required. In this discussion we presented scientific approaches for developing and writing syllabi of IT education in schools.

3.2 Importance of computer education in Schools

Computer technology or IT plays a vital role in our daily life. In each sector of our life we face the importance of computer technology. IT made the communication and overall life easy. The same like other subject students in schools needs to learn how to interact with technological aspects. In school students must have the ability to know how IT related devices work and how they can be used.

The learning of computer education influences students to solve their problems in other subjects like math, biology and else. Computer education is an influence factor for learning other subjects. Students who gain the knowledge of IT education and Computer Science will be able to know how a machine work and will try to think on further aspects which don't exist. This indeed helps students in abstract thinking. Computer education has the practical base for learning. Whatever students learn, they can implement it practically. They get the ability to implement the academic principle in the real world system. [25]

The same like other subjects computer science have it is own theoretical concepts and mathematical understanding behinds it. Hence, students learn the logics, reasoning and constructive thinking. The discussion describing the importance of computer science in [25] which is certified by BCS, Microsoft, Google and Intellect is concluded as follow:

"The combination of computational thinking, a set of computing principles, and a computational approach to problem solving is uniquely empowering. The ability to bring this combination to bear on practical problems is central to the success of science, engineering, business and commerce in the 21st century."

However, Computer Science and IT are complementary of each other but still they can't be called the same. Computer Science reflects the purpose and how the computer works, while IT reflects the usage of the computer. In our case our aim is to train our children to have their role in all aspects of the technological life. Although all citizens will be able to use different technological devices and systems, but those who attends schools must know the computational concepts behind them. [25] Therefore, the syllabi which we discussed in coming sections encompass both computer science and IT.

3.3 Concept verses application based syllabus

However, the title for this section represents the comparison of two types of syllabi but at first here is a glance to the history of school syllabus for computer education in developed countries.

In the start, in the USA computer education was started as subject of computer literacy in which computer programming was included. Later on the policy maker turn their attention to the usage of different software in education system. They focused to computer as a practical tool rather than a computing machine in education. In Germany and Japan the main focus was on teaching programing, even though in secondary general education. In UK and France the emphasis was on Computer Assisted Instruction, while in France the possibility was given to students aged 15 or more to attend some programming classes. [26]

In France the committee which was assigned to find the solution for the curriculum of computer literacy decided to focus on application based syllabi rather than concrete technical concepts. They held a full year academic training for the teachers of 530 schools in computer science. Almost 5000 teachers attended this course in the year from 1970 to 1976. The course was designed to focus more on technical concepts of computer programming and algorithms, while the curriculum for computer education was in different approach. This training raised some unwanted results. The participants of the course learned that playing with machine is easy and interesting rather than explaining boring theoretical concepts. A variety of participants found the learning of programming difficult. Hence, negligible number of the participant got the idea to include technical computer programming concept in the curriculum. [26]

In the UK, "The National Development Program in Computer Assisted Learning (NDPCAL)" finally set two objectives to achieve overall in computer literacy. Computer Aided Learning (CAL) and Computer Managed Instruction (CMI). The above institution funded several project for achieving both objectives. The first objective was set to focus more on Computer technical concepts, while the second objective was focusing on computer as education aided tool. [26] In the conclusion about the start of Computer Education in UK we can write that, they agreed to implement both approaches in parallel.

In curriculum of Computer Science in India; emphasizes is on learning of concepts which can be implemented with different tools, instead of learning the usage of specific tool or application. The curriculum need to be dynamic and should include information about the advent and usage of new tools, while in parallel it should focus on conceptual learning. [27]

In [27] the curriculum for computer education is divided into three categories of Concepts, Usage Skills and Social Aspects. The mixture of these three categories must be considered for different aged group. In Concepts syllabi should be written about computer fundamental operation or usage/function. In Usage Skills syllabi should cover different hardware or software usage like IT tools, Communication tools, Technology research tools and problem solving tools. And finally the last category of Social Aspects must focus on security related issues of computer and Internet.

Dr. Viera Krnanová Proulx a Computer Science Associate Professor at Northeastern University propose that syllabi for Computer Education at schools period should cover the following five concepts of computing: Representation of data; learning about an algorithm as a set of instructions; looking at computer as a machine that carries out the algorithm; teaching students to discover new algorithms and analyze them; and examining different algorithm based problem solving strategies.[28]

In primary and secondary schools, if students learn algorithms, they will be able to think and find different ideas for a problem. In Computer Science concepts, there are different solutions and algorithms for a problem, while in other subjects students must follow predefined formulas or limited solutions. These indeed give the chance of freedom to school students to think freely and invent new ideas. [28]

The matter of preferring concept verses application based syllabi for computer education is always discussing issues and it differed in each country in the start and now. In article [26] the main reasons on discussion of computer education syllabi are outlined follow:

a) Computer is (will be) everywhere (in the future) and students must learn how to use them.

b) Programming and other theoretical concepts like logics and algorithms have cultural impacts so they must be the compulsory part of syllabi.

In the view of the above two arguments, we can conclude that for different age students a mixture of both concept and application based syllabi should be developed. For further understanding the goals of concept based curriculum some terms are defined here to explain different process which students must learn in computer education in school.

3.3.1 Computational Thinking

The computational thinking is done by the people where they must have the ability to think logically, algorithmically, recursively and abstractly rather computers. The computational thinking is defined in [25] as follow:

28

"Computational thinking is the process of recognizing aspects of computation in the world that surrounds us, and applying tools and techniques from computing to understand and reason about both natural and artificial systems and processes."

3.3.2 Abstraction

In computational thinking the scale and complexity of the systems that is studied or build is managed by abstraction. The abstraction includes specific forms, like modeling, decomposing, and generalizing. Where, complexity is hidden by simple abstraction which has complicated details in the background. For example, a procedure supports abstraction by hiding the complex details of an implementation behind a simple interface. [25]

3.3.3 Modeling

The representation of a real world issue, system or situation which covers all specification and details of that system is called modeling. However, it is required to have different modeling for different purposes, but particular situation may also require more than one model. [25]

3.3.4 Decomposing

The process of splitting a problem into sub-problems and finding solutions for each sub-problem and merging the sub-solution to solve the original problem is called decomposing. For example, a graph which show the topology of the network and explain different components of a network like client, server, and network and the way they communicate with each other, is good way to understand the whole network system. [25]

3.3.5 Generalizing and classifying

The share specification between different examples or to find general specification of a complexity is called generalizing. In this way by explicitly finding share and different aspects of a specific example; complexity is solved. [25]

3.3.6 Programming

However, programming is a subset of Computer Science, but it is absolutely central process for Computer Science. Programming in educational purpose is defined in [25] as follow:

"Programming encourages creativity, logical thought, precision and problem-solving, and helps foster the personal, learning and thinking skills required in the modern school curriculum. Programming gives concrete, physical form to the idea of "abstraction", and repeatedly shows how useful it is."

3.3.7 Debugging, testing, and reasoning about programs

The process of fixing a programmed system is called debugging. The programming skills give the ability to students to develop systematic approach to solve the problem and test the different programmed system. Where students learn to read the documentation, explain how the code works, execute code in draft paper, find the problem and isolate them, add comments and finally they learn how to choose test cases. [25]

3.4 Syllabuses for Computer Education at School

The question of what concepts should be covered in the school period arises? In [25] the concepts which are necessary to be covered in the school as computer education subject are divided into six sections. They developed curriculum for differed age and then outlined the different topics from the mentioned six sections for each age group which is called Key Stage. Their curriculum is well-known standard curriculum in London and is approved by several companies which invest and deal with computer technology. Hence, we present the abstract of the syllabi which they outlined.

- **Algorithm:** Students must know what algorithm is and how it is used. Different types of algorithm and its representation via charts. The usage of condition and loops in algorithm and other concepts.

- **Programs:** Students must get the ability to use at least one programming language and he/she must be able to write and execute small programs.
- **Data:** How data is represented (binary representation), stored (Tables, Column and Rows), transmitted, and organized. Data types (Integers, Binary, Hexdecimal and etc.)
- **Computers:** Students must know how is computer made and what devices operate to gather to make computer system. Computer Hardware and its usage, further concepts of logic gates, operating systems and etc.
- **Communication and the Internet:** The [Input>Process>Output] concept, Network, Internet, Protocols (TCP/IP, HTTP), routing and switching concepts.
- **Optional topics for advanced students:** Some advance computing concepts can be added for optional studies to the higher class of schools.

The above listed section for each topic can be added to the syllabi of different grades and further details can be written based on them. Further topics of Computer usage and its social impacts can also be added to syllabi. The students should be able to use computer for webbing, text editing, drawings, presenting and calculation. They must be able to use Internet for different purposes. The concepts for doing research and composing them via computer are also necessities for students at schools.

3.5 Security Concepts and Privacy

It is highly recommended to include security concepts in syllabi for schools. Teenagers are a vulnerable group of targets which is highly affected by security threat from IT or social media. The matter of threats and risks from IT arises in both offline and online technologies. Greater attention has to be given to online technologies. As stated earlier in the article [27], the syllabi of schools are divided into three parts, where the last part discussed the social impacts of technology.

Specifically, for online threats, we can say that online communication and business is one of the key aspects of today's life. Many people are using online resources for their activities and entertainment. Although Internet and overall online services provide significant facilities to human beings, there are still some concerns which should be taken into consideration when using online services.

The most important and challenging concern that affects online users is misuse of private information. Privacy is an important issue that affects our daily life; the digital age made privacy a very important concern for the people. By introducing social communication sites like Facebook, people's concerns about privacy issues had increased. Therefore, it is necessary to provide more information to the students in school whom are a main target group of intruders.

With the progress of technology, protecting and violating privacy has changed dramatically. As new technologies are being introduced, its vulnerabilities have created new privacy dilemmas for the society. Many new ways for gathering private information are occurring due to the vulnerabilities of these technologies. One of the most important and challenging problems in electronic age is to protect privacy.

The Internet is potentially affecting privacy, which has introduced new concerns. Usually, computers used to access Internet can permanently store records of everything. "Where every online photo, status update, and Twitter post and blog entry by and about us can be stored forever," writes law professor and author Jeffrey Rosen.[1]

It should be explicitly described to students that privacy issues can damage their social career and they must know what to protect and how to protect it to be safe. According to a report from Microsoft, 75 percent of U.S. employers search about their applicants online in social networking sites; they are mostly using information which can be found through search engines, social networking sites, personal web sites and blogs, and Twitter or Facebook. It is claimed that 70 percent of all applications are rejected based on Internet information. [29]

Privacy is an important issue, which every online and offline user must pay attention to. It is very important to have in mind that everything that is shared online can possibly be seen by the general public. It means what you share on Facebook or any other social web

---

[1]http://www.nytimes.com/2010/07/25/magazine/25privacy-t2.html?_r=1&adxnnl=1&ref= technology &adxnnlx=1326457540-AlfJC3Vhg4EW1bVL6mUgyw

site is potentially public and your competitors may use your pictures, videos, information and thoughts against you. Whatever is shared can be used for social engineering or cyber bullying, and it can have harmful consequences for online users. There are many examples of privacy being threatened which is a lesson to learn from for the users who are careless when it comes to privacy issues. [2]

There is tremendous power in social media as it connects people of various backgrounds. But individuals can be good or bad users, so it is important that users are made aware of this to not being targeted. This is the responsibility of online social networks administrators to help its user for protecting their privacy.

Students should know that all online resources, especially social websites, should be modeled for appropriate use. Steps to be taken include to completely signing out of everything you are not using. A better management will decrease the risks and harms. The concepts of digital vulnerabilities, online safety, ethical behavior and cyber bullying should be taught to students in schools. In addition, it is important to explain privacy settings of different online social networks.

Furthermore, students must know how to deal with their stored data and how to keep it secret. They must know that their stored data is stored forever and after deletion it can be restored again. The harms that can arise in a culturally sensitive society like Afghanistan should be explained to the students.

Afghanistan is a multi-culture, multi-nation and multi-religion country. Each ethnic and tribe has their own culture and way of dealing with society. However, all have some shared characteristics in common. Information technology increased the risks of cultural problems. Mr. Wali Achakzai, an Afghan author identified some problems that are caused by IT deployment [30]. Broadcasting negative and violated speech toward other nations, tribes with the help of IT caused loss of trust and unification among the people. According to a report from BBC Pashto, three females were killed in the border area of Afghanistan, only because of publishing a video on the Internet which was recorded via mobile by someone (May 2012). In Afghan Culture it is highly prohibited to share family information

---

[2] http://mashable.com/2009/10/10/facebook-poke-arrest/

with the public, but with growth of online social network (OSN), especially Facebook, all information is public, which caused many problems in the society. There are several cases reported that sharing names, photos or videos of any female or male caused family problems, like divorce or even death. These all issues should be covered in the syllabi of the schools so that teenagers who are the victim of misuse of technology get aware of it and learn how to protect their privacy.

3.6 Open Source concepts

The Open Source term covers broader aspects than Software. The overall idea of Openness describes the freedom of the users for creation, recoding, distributing and using of production. This production either can be a Software program or content which can be accessible to the user for free via Internet or other resource. These products can be used, redistribute and modify freely under the guarantee of specific Software license. In all open source products source code and compiled version should be available. [31]

The Open Source idea for content can be exemplified in Wikipedia which is available online (http://www.wikipedia.org) to all Internet users. It describes the idea to access information and share your knowledge with others. All users can use the available information from Wikipedia or can either upload new or edit existence information. In this way the ability of volunteer team work is expressed. However, information in Wikipedia can't be cite as scientific arguments, but is huge network of volunteer for creating content almost about everything.

The Open Source Software that can be called free Software is the cheapest way to use the benefits of technology. Although the terms Open Source Software and Free Software can be used interchangeably, but the term Open Source means the availability of the code with the product for the user to modify, use, read and redistribute it under a Software license. [32]

Open Source Software (OSS) or Free/Libre Open Source Software (F/LOSS) is a type of Software system. The Open Source expresses the availability of the code with the program and Free or Libre means the freedom of the consumer which has the right to use, read, modify and distribute the code and the product.

The Open Source products have variety of advantages over other type of products in school. The most important benefit for the school infrastructure is the economic advantage of Open Source. All computer machines in lab can run Open Source Operating System (e.g. Linux) and there are different applications available that runs over Linux platform which can be used for different educational purposes. This indeed reduces the cost of proprietary software license. [32]

The Open Source community is developed based on volunteer work, where individuals across the world contribute to community for developing different Open Source application. Hence, if student learn how is Open Source working and how the community is managed. They will gain the chance to implement their theoretical knowledge in team work in Open Source community by developing applications. The students will get experience in team work and will have the ability to solve the problem in a real environment. [33] Overall students will find its work in the real application used by everyone. This will encourage him to participate in volunteer work and make his professional career.

In case study [34] the benefits of Open Source in education is emphasized as follow:

"It is nonetheless our opinion that the real benefit of open source and open content in general relies not on the cost factor but on the ideology behind it. We argue that opening up education increases the availability of high quality ready to use content."

To conclude the discussion, it is important to have information about Open Source products in the syllabi. Open Source beside its other advantages, it is part of Computer Science concepts and student must learn these concepts. In Afghanistan where economy is low, and infrastructure is going to be built newly, this is a good motivation to use Open Source instead investing on proprietary software.

3.6.1 Proprietary Software and current syllabus

Proprietary software is developed by a specific company or group which has the property or ownership of that software. This means no individuals or users have the right to access, read, modify the code and distribute the product. It is almost the opposite of Open Source. The license for every proprietary software product should be purchased.

In current syllabi of Computer Education in Afghans Schools as stated in the previous section the usage of few outdated proprietary software are covered (e.g. Microsoft Windows XP, Microsoft Office 2003 Packages).

There are few reasons which decrease the value of the content; these applications are outdated and not used anymore today or in the time when the books were printed and published. Hence, our argument for focusing on theoretical concepts rather application usage is strengthening. These applications are Proprietary and there is no discussion about the license of its usage and publishing its usage guide as syllabi for school. This indeed encourages the students to use these applications, where the economy is low even in governmental side all computer in school will equip with illegal instead of licensed software. The same for personal computer in student's family; all will use illegal software. Therefore we claim that the current syllabi open a backdoor to the usage of illegal products.

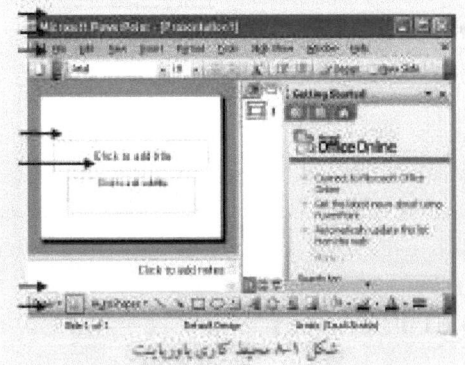

Figure 12 Proprietary software in currenty syllabi

36

The Figure 12 Proprietary software in currenty syllabi is snipped from page 80 of the computer education book for 11th grade. This figure illustrates the window of Microsoft PowerPoint. However, this book was print and published in 2011 but the content is too outdated.

Open Source Community have variety of different software products which can be used for different purposes. Hence, it is highly recommended to instruct the usage of Open Source application in computer education syllabi as part of computer usage instead of proprietary software.

Fourth Chapter

In this chapter we focus on teachers for computer education in schools. As stated in previous sections lack of professional teachers is a challenging problem that affects overall education process in Afghanistan. We tried to study the experience in other country and present our solution in context of Afghanistan.

4.1 Computer education teachers' proficiency

In successful implementation of curriculum proficiency of teachers play a vital role. In [35] it is stated that computer education teachers in schools should be able to reflect technical knowledge correctly and reliably; and have teaching skills, to provide perspective for grasping the interest of the students.

The hiring and retraining process of teachers for computer education in schools is very problematic, because the amount of salary paid to computer teachers is too low then other computer scientists who serve as industrials and there are no sufficient teacher training programs to promote the skills of new teachers. [36]

The proficiency of teacher for teaching computer science is reflected to the knowledge of teacher in technical aspects, pedagogical disciplines and Socio-cultural knowledge. Teachers who serve as computer education teachers in school must have technical background in computer science. They must know the basics and fundamentals of computer science and it requires for them to know the methodology of teaching technical concepts. They must know how to present different concepts to the students and how to make students to learn these aspects. Overall, for their co-assistance it is required to be part of teachers association to get experience from teaching of other expert teachers. In this way they will gain more professional experience and will gain the ability to present the courses in professional way. [35]

Those teachers who gain technical knowledge and pedagogical disciplines, they must have the chance to do practical teaching before working as a teacher in school. In this way the gap between the theoretical knowledge that they got during their studies and practical environment in the school will be filled and will become professional teachers. [35]

In [36] a quote is written from administrators of Dallas Independent School District in USA that says:

"We continue to get more computer equipment each year, but finding teachers with expertise to use the equipment is a difficult task…"

This indeed is more difficult in Afghanistan, where overall computer science and technology are newly evolving fields. Hence, government and policy makers must grasp there broader attention to teacher training programs.

4.2 Teachers training

Teacher training is the most important program for improving computer education. In [36] the authors described the teacher training program very important for computer education and they focused on training of teachers for computer education into three categories. The in-service computer science teacher's training, pre-service courses and teacher certification program in computer are three categories proposed in the mentioned paper.

The training program for currently employed teachers which is named retraining of computer education teachers, aims to update and strengthen the technical and methodological knowledge of the teachers [37]. The author propose to conduct yearly 5 to 6 days training for teachers to deliver them new update in technical world of computer science (like new programming languages and features).

In Afghanistan currently the only institution offering bachelor in computer education as teaching field is Kabul Education University (KEU). However, the curriculum of this institution is also not well defined to fill the demand of computer education teachers in the market. In interview with Head of Computer Department in KEU, he stated their department graduates average 60 students as teachers yearly. [20] However, all graduated students are not joining schools as computer teachers only half of them work as computer teachers in schools.

In Ministry of Education the department of teacher training doesn't have the section for training computer education teachers. The second biggest institution offering two year certification in teacher training is Sayed Jamal-ul-Din Afghan Teacher Training Institute. This institute while our visit in Jan 2013 didn't had teacher training program for computer education. Although it is to mention that a computer department was operating, but they were only offering short term computer usage courses to other departments. There are several other teacher training institutions in all provinces of Afghanistan, but none of them were offering courses or certification in computer education teacher training.

The teacher training process is the most important part of computer education improvement plan. Therefore, Ministry of Education must create a department of computer education teacher training in Teacher training directorate. This department should get the responsibility of coordinating computer education teacher training programs.

This department should conduct surveys for optimizing the needs and status of computer education teachers. Based on the findings of the survey the must make their annual plan for teacher training program. The teacher training plan must focus on two categories of training programs.

The first categories of programs must focus on current computer education teachers whom are not professional and don't have computer science knowledge. In these programs the concept of in-service studies which exist for other fields can be consider. In the in-service concepts teachers can continue their teaching and in the meantime they must obtain certification in computer education teacher training.

The concepts of retraining stated in [37] can also be counted in the first category of programs. The short trainings, workshops, symposiums or seminars should be conducted in different province all over Afghanistan. This indeed strengthens the collaborations between computer education teachers and will gain updated knowledge about the content they are delivering.

The second categories of programs must focus on new teacher training institution. The Computer Science Department in Kabul Education University that offer bachelor degree in computer education teacher training must increase the number of students. It is highly recommended to increase the number of graduated students from 50 to 200 yearly. In the meanwhile the number of institutions offering the same degree overall in Afghanistan should be expanded. Due to lack of resources, it won't be possible to offer certification in computer education teacher training in all provinces, but zone province (Kandahar, Herat, Nangarhar, Balkh and Kabul) must have at least one institute offering the degree. The second biggest institute Sayed Jamal-ul-Din Afghan Teacher Training Institute must create computer education teacher training department. This covers both in-service students and regular students.

The department of computer education teacher training in Ministry of Education must also work to create a teachers union. In [37] it is stated that; this type of union or association will gather the computer education teachers and will make the opportunity for them to share their experience and focus on different sides of computer education.

The curriculum for the teacher training programs is also a discussing issue. The mentioned department in Ministry of Education must make sure to have unified and updated curriculum in all institutions offering computer education teacher training. This curriculum has to be based on curriculum developed for computer education in schools. It must cover both technical knowledge and methodology of teaching technical concepts.

In [36] the problem of salary paid to computer education teachers versus industrial computer scientists is raised. To eliminate the problem in Afghanistan the law of civilian services deployed by the Administration Reforms Commission says: *"Those who obtain degree or certification in teacher training will not be hired in other sectors of government. They can only work as teachers in schools."* However, this is a restriction for eliminating the problem but the private markets have broader chances to these computer education graduates. Hence, government should consider paying higher or equal salary for the teacher of computer education and other industrials computer scientist. Government can make further motivation to join schools as teachers (Like providing them house for living).

Fifth Chapter

In this chapter we focus on infrastructure for computer education in schools. In the previous sections we have explained that Afghan schools don't have proper infrastructure in schools to deliver computer education. However, the process of development and reconstruction is rapidly growing in Afghanistan, but here we focus on specific required infrastructure for computer education.

5.1 Infrastructure for computer education in schools

In computer education after the most important aspects discussed earlier like syllabi and professional teachers, the next important factor for improving computer education is infrastructure. If we have well-defined and standard syllabi and professional teachers, but don't have required infrastructure still we are not able to improve the current situation.

In article [38] the whole computer learning system is illustrate in a Cartesian product. This illustration best fit the computer learning system. It is shown in the figure below:

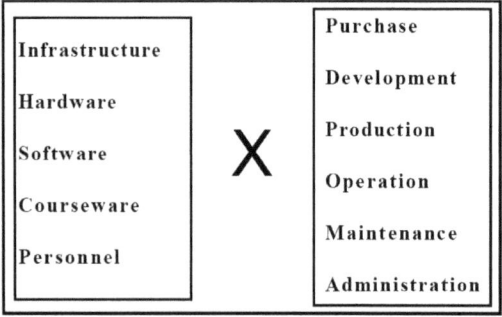

Figure 13 Computer Learning Component

The above Cartesian product explains several think very well. We can get several "don'ts" from these illustrations which are also discussed in the original paper. Don't buy computer without having professional teachers, don't start project without assuring the

42

long term budget for maintenance and operation, and don't waste time on small project with big plans. These indeed show us that we should consider the whole set for implementing and improving computer education.

In situation of Afghanistan the following idea is a good argument to consider while developing curriculum for computer education. The main emphasis of computer education curriculum should be on thinking and learning how to solve problems, that needs few computer facilities. This option makes the opportunities for students to learn computer in schools that lack standard and required infrastructure. [28]

The problem of infrastructure for computer education in schools of Afghanistan is challenging matter. We have tried to discuss these issues and present our solutions. The discussion on infrastructure is divided to several parts. Here we focus on some administrative problems and in coming titles we discuss electricity, lab and hardware.

The computer education is not recognized officially as department in school by the Ministry of Education. In most of the schools it is a part of English language department. [17] Though, it is part of subjects defined in the curriculum of mentioned Ministry. [21] This means that Ministry of Education developed syllabi and add this subject to the curriculum of schools but still don't have budget to add it to the administrative structure of every school. This problem should be solved by Ministry of Education. Computer Education should have its own separate department.

The teaching time for computer education is limited to three appointments of 35 minutes per week. [19] This timing is not only for lecture, it includes time for administrative issues like attendance and etc. In this period of time student must change the class and get to Computer Lab. Hence, only 25 minutes will be left for each lecture. This is too less. Hopefully administration in Ministry of Education will consider this important and will extend it to two appointments of 120 minutes per week.

5.2 Electricity

In discussion of infrastructure the first important and required matter is the availability of electricity to power up computer machinery or hardware. However, Afghanistan has sufficient resource to provide non-stop electricity for all citizens and organizations, but lack of investment on those resources caused to have electricity for short period of time in few cities. This affects the situation of computer education in schools. Majority of schools across Afghanistan are lacking access to electricity. Some schools in cities specifically schools located in capital Kabul have non-stop electricity, while schools in other major cities like Herat, Kandahar, Nangarhar and Balkh have access to electricity only for short period of time weekly. This is different in urban areas and less developed provinces.

To overcome the problem the solar technology is experienced in some schools in Kandahar, Herat and Nangarhar by government and some funding agencies. [17] In our survey we have found that these schools have good experience from using this technology. As solar penal are installed in these schools and operate to power up computer labs and other administration in the school independently so the problem of maintenance and protection of the equipment while not having technical staff arises. Overall schools using this technology are happy with their experience and welling to expand the capacity of panels. They recommend implementing the solar technology in other schools too.

The Afghan government in their overall strategic plan should give priority to investment on electricity resources. Electricity and power is the main factor for development in each sector. To overcome the problem in current situation we propose some temporary solutions. The current electricity available in some cities should be distributed to schools and priority in the time table should be given to schools operating time.

A governmental commission should study the availability of less required budgets resource of electricity to power up schools. The experience of solar panel in some schools can be expanded to other schools. The maintenance and protection plan for solar panels and their power production system should be developed. Ministry of Education with close relation to Ministry of Energy and Water should work on providing power or electricity to Afghan Schools. It is highly recommended to assign a directorate to manage the maintenance, protection and distribution of power or electricity to schools in Ministry of Education.

The directorate should study the budget for power generator and solar panel for different schools and then decide and implement projects for powering up the schools. However, we recommend city electricity to expand to all schools, but looks this is not practical in short term. Therefore, we encourage investing on solar panel rather than on power generator. The experience of power generator in some schools shows that they are not happy cause of not having sufficient budget for fuel. The power generator also causes environmental pollution.

5.3 Practical Lab

However, practical computer labs in schools are less challenging in the case of Afghanistan, because majority of schools have building only few schools in urban areas and less developed province don't have prober building. This means almost every school has facility to allocate a room or class as computer lab. In our study we found that the room allocated for computer machine are stores rather than regular class, therefore we recommend to have at least two computer labs and a store for keeping computer related tools. However, if we don't have required computer machine for the school too, still allocation of lab will help as future facility.

5.4 Hardware equipment

The hardware equipment in school is problematic issue of Afghan School. Overall, the lack of sufficient budget causes to invest less in this part. In schools that computer machinery and other required hardware are available, face the problem of maintaining and protection. In majority of schools existing hardware are not operating and they are stored. Hence, besides investing on hardware a policy for maintaining and protection is required.

Afghanistan is a developing country and facing the limitation of budget to invest more in each sector. Therefore the experience of using cheap hardware in school for computer education is preferred idea. In [39] the two low-cost computer technology is discussed.

The "One-laptop-per-child" (OLPC) aims to provide low cost computer for every school going age child in developing countries. This technology uses low-cost computers operating on open source (XO) operating system and consumes low power. The cost of every single computer is up to 175 USD and connected to the network through wireless mesh technology. Individuals can't buy single machine, only governments can invest on for whole school compasses. However, the Afghan government invested on this technology [11], but the project is implemented in few schools in some province and currently it is stopped.

The next technology discussed in mentioned paper [39] is "N-Computing". This technology work based on sharing concept, where a computer shares its resource and timing to several users in schools. In this method 30 students can access computer using accessing equipment like keyboard, mouse and monitor. Overall, the same like OPLC in this method every student can have its own computer, but in fact opposite OPLC its one PC. So in one class a single PC provide facility for 30 students. This indeed is cheaper for implementing, where it cost 70 USD per student.

There are other technologies also offering low-cost computer for developing countries and there is broader attention in this field to develop cheapest technologies. Indian tries to develop laptops costs 35$ which will change the debate. [39]

The computer markets offer different variety of computers which has to survey and then decide to purchase for Afghan Schools. The refurbish and used computers are also good option to buy them and then renovate them. This require fewer budgets then purchasing the brand models.

The concept of sharing a simple or regular PC by several students can also cover the problem. However, this makes some students active while other students sharing the same PC get passive. Hence, all students don't have the chance to use the benefit of available stations. To solve the problem the idea of using multiple mice (mouse) for single PC is addressed in [40]. The authors introduced the idea of using multiple mice with different curser color for single PC. In this method all students sharing single PC can take part in educational content and games actively. In their efforts they tried to develop software to support different colored cursers and other educational applications. Although multiple mice are supported in windows for single curser by plugging several mice through USB, but the aim of the authors is several mice with several colored curser. The figure below shows their efforts.

Figure 14 Snapshot of educational software with multiple colored cursers

After considering the type of computer machine before purchasing them the matter of maintenance and protection of these products should also be considered. We recommend having at least one technical staff that has to take care of damage hardware and take the responsibility of maintenance and periodic checkup. The software updates and digital security should also be considered as his responsibility. This technical staff can be called an IT officer in each school.

Conclusion

Computer Education is an important subject in schools and needs further research. In our work, we conducted a survey and analyzed the current computer education situation in Afghan schools. We did research based on our finding and present it in our thesis.

The current computer education situation in Afghanistan is not sufficient and requires broader attention of policy makers and scientists. We have found that a close coordination among the Ministry of Education, Ministry of Higher Education, Academy of Science of Afghanistan and Ministry of Information and Communication is required to develop standard and national curriculum for computer education in schools.

The first step to starts improving computer education is to write an action plan for it. We believe that this plan should contains strategies for teacher proficiency, syllabi renewal and infrastructure development.

In syllabi renewal; a committee of computer scientists and professionals should be assigned to work close with computer science and IT faculties across Afghanistan. They should rewrite the syllabi for 10th, 11th and 12th grade and should write the new syllabi for 7th, 8th and 9th grade. The syllabi should focus on computer science and computer usage both. The concepts of digital security and open source community should also be included in the syllabi.

In teacher proficiency; the teacher training directorate in the Ministry of Education must create a department for computer education teacher training. This department should work on planning for teacher training. The teacher training program should be implemented in two categories. The first category contains plan for in-service training. This type of training should be held for the teacher whom are currently involved in teaching process but are not professional of computer science. The knowledge update or integration with new changes in computer science short term training can also be categorized to this part. The second category contains plan for regular students, this help to train computer science teachers for schools. For the co-assistance among teachers a computer education teachers association is proposed.

In infrastructure; the electricity resource for schools should be study by a directorate which is defined in our thesis. The experience of solar panel installation in schools should be expanded to other schools after the study of mentioned directorate. In each school at least two class rooms should be allocated as computer labs. The different solution of the hardware presented in our thesis can be considered in practice. Our recommendation is to invest on Personal Computers (PC) and share strategy for usage. The required software definition for sharing a single tool is also part of syllabi writing and development committee responsibility.

The maintenance and protection of hardware and assuring latest software and security essentials requires a technical staff at each school. Hence, we recommend hiring a staff as IT officer in each school.

To start the improvement of computer education we propose to implement different pilot projects. As sample once school in each of major cities should get equip with require infrastructure and hardware. These schools can work as computer education facility providing coordination center. The teacher training courses, seminar or workshop can be held in these pre-equip schools.

In this way we will be able to improve computer education in schools all over Afghanistan. In the end, it was our pleasure to work on this project as our Master thesis in TU-Berlin. In one side, we accomplished what we wanted and in the other side, we were able to present solutions to the problems of our developing country (Afghanistan).

References

[1] P. Colonel Eugene J. Palka, Afghanistan a regional geography, New York: United States Military Academy, 2001.

[2] Afghanistan in Perspective: An orientation guide, Defence Language Institute Foreign Language Center, 2012.

[3] *Constituation of Afghanistan,* Kabul: Independent Commision for Overseeing the implementation of constituation, 2003.

[4] A. Featherstone, "Afghanistan: A case study," Europion Union, Humantarian Policy Group Norwegian Refugee Council, 2012.

[5] H. Fischer, "Education in Afghanistan," German Embassy, Kabul, 2011.

[6] D. S. A. Zarifi, " نوی ښوونیز نصاب، خانګرتیاوي، نیمګرتیاوي او راتلونکي هیلی)New Educational Curriculum, specification, drawbacks and future welling)," Ministry of Education, Kabul, 2012.

[7] "Infrastructure," USAID-Afghansitan, Kabul, 2006.

[8] A. R. Samadi, "Energy consumption and available energy resources in Afghanistan," June 2011. [Online]. Available: http://www.usea.org/sites/default/files/event-file/522/Afghan_Power_Sector_Briefing_June_2011.pdf. [Accessed May 2013].

[9] A. M. Mohmand, A. Marjan and A. Sangin, "Developing e-Government in Afghanistan," in *ICEGOV '10 4th International Conference on Theory and Practice of Electronic Governance*, New York, 2010.

[10] W. Larry, K. Frank and S. Stuart, "Information and Communication Technologies for Reconstruction and Development Afghanistan Challenges and Opportunities," Center for Technology and National Security Policy National Defense University, Washington DC, 2008.

[11] "OLPC Afghanistan/Deployment News," One Laptop Per Child, 29 May 2013. [Online]. Available: http://wiki.laptop.org/go/OLPC_Afghanistan/Deployment_News. [Accessed 8 June 2013].

[12] K. Egan, "What Is Curriculum?," *Curriculum Inquiry,* vol. 8, no. 1, p. 65, 1978.

[13] J. W. Bloom, "Selected Concepts of Curriculum," 2006.

[14] D. G. Oblinger, Game Changers Education and Information Technology, Educause, 2012.

[15] N. Peroz, Framework for a Functional IT Supply in Higher Education in Afghanistan, Berlin: LIT Verlag, 2009.

[16] "Computer Education," Help the Afghan Children, 2012. [Online]. Available: http://www.helptheafghanchildren.org/pages.aspx?content=27. [Accessed 12 June 2013].

[17] S. Administrators, Interviewee, *Computer Education for Afghan Schools (Questioner for schools administrators).* [Interview]. 2012.

[18] "Education is the Future Rebuilding Higher Education in Afghanistan," DAAD (Deutscher Akademischer Austaucsh Dienst), Germany, 2012.

[19] S. Teachers, Interviewee, *Computer Education for Afghan Schools (Questioner for schools teachers).* [Interview]. 2012.

[20] S. Barakzai, Interviewee, *Teacher Training Facilities in KEU.* [Interview]. 19 November 2012.

[21] نصاب تعليمي معارف افغانستان(Afghanistan's Educational Curriculum), Kabul: Ministry of Education, 2011.

[22] T. M. Wahadyar and R. Zaheer, کمپیوتر د یوولسم ټولګي لپاره(Computer for 11th Grade), Kabul: Ministry of Education, 2011.

[23] T. M. Wahadyar and R. Zaheer, کمپیوتر د دولسم ټولګي لپاره(Computer for 12th Grade), Kabul: Ministry of Education, 2011.

[24] T. M. Wahadyar and R. Zaheer, کمپیوتر د لسم ټولګي لپاره(Computer for 10th Grade), Kabul: Ministry of Education, 2011.

[25] "Computer Science: A curriculum for schools," Computing at School Working Group, London, 2012.

[26] J. Hebenstreit, "Computer in Education in Developed Countries Methods, Achivement and Problems," United Nations Educational Scientific and Cultural Organization,

Paris, 1984.

[27] M. Baru, S. Iyer and U. Bellur, "Computer Science Curriculum for Schools," Sri Sri Ravishankar Vidya Mandir (SSRVM), Bangalore, 2007.

[28] D. V. K. Proulx, "Computer Science in Elementary and Secondary Schools," Northeastern University, Boston.

[29] "The Web Means the End of Forgetting," The New York Times, 21 07 2010. [Online]. Available: http://www.nytimes.com/2010/07/25/magazine/25privacy-t2.html?_r=1&adxnnl=1&ref=technology&adxnnlx=1326457540-AlfJC3Vhg4EW1bVL6mUgyw. [Accessed 13 01 2012].

[30] W. Achakzai, "Pay attention to the risks of Internet," Tolafghan, 01 July 2011. [Online]. Available: http://www.tolafghan.com/posts/22041. [Accessed 02 July 2012].

[31] D. P. Carmichael and M. L. Honour, "Open Source as Appropriate Technology for Global Education," *International Journal of Educational Development,* vol. 22, no. 1, pp. 47-53, January 2002.

[32] K. J. O'Hara and J. S. Kay, "Open Source Software and Computer Science Education," *J. Comput. Sci. Coll.,* vol. 18, no. 3, pp. 1-7, February 2003.

[33] G. W. Hislop, H. J. C. Ellis, A. B. Tucker and S. Dexter, "Using open source software to engage students in computer science education," *SIGCSE Bull.,* vol. 41, no. 1, p. 134–135, March 2009.

[34] A. Brocco and F. Frapolli, "Open Source in Higher Education: Case Study Computer Science at the University of Fribourg," University of Fribourg, Fribourg, 2011.

[35] C. Stephenson, J. Gal-Ezer, B. Haberman and A. Verno, "The New Educational Imperative: Improving High School Computer Science Education," Computer Science Teachers Association, New York, 2006.

[36] J. L. Poirot, "Computer education in the secondary school: Problems and solutions," in *SIGCSE '79 Proceedings of the tenth SIGCSE technical symposium on Computer science education*, New York, 1979.

[37] J. L. POIROT, H. G. TAYLOR and C. A. NORRIS, "Retraining teachers to teach high school computer science," *Communications of the ACM,* vol. 31, no. 7, pp. 912-917, 1988.

[38] L. Osin, "Computers in Education in Developing Countries: Why and How?," *Education and Technology Series,* vol. 3, no. 1, 1998.

[39] J. James, "Low-Cost Computers for Education in Developing," *Social Indicators Research ,* vol. 103, no. 3, pp. 399-408, 2011.

[40] U. S. Pawar, J. Pal and K. Toyama, "Multiple Mice for Computers in Education in Developing Countries," in *Information and Communication Technologies and Development*, Berkeley, 2006.

Appendixes

Appendix I: Summary of School's Administrator survey

Summary of Suvery about Computer Education with Administrators of Schools in Afghanistan

No	Name of School	Province	Teachers		Students		Computer Lab	Computer Library	Devices availabe in school							
			Male	Female	Male	Female			PC	Laptop	Server	Printer	Switch	Router	Power Hub	Data Hub
1	Batti Koot	Nangarhar	1		300		1		7			1			7	
2	Saifi Girls School	Herat		2		500	1		5						5	
3	Amankhail	Nangarhar	1		1500				8						8	
4	Shahid Arif	Nangarhar	1	2	2400	656	1	1	11						11	
5	Hawza Karbaz	Herat		2		210	1	1	10			1			10	
6	Babashi	Herat		2		150	1	1								
7	Alayee	Nangarhar		3	600		2	1	37						37	
8	Ahmad Shah Baba	Kandahar	2		600			1	17						17	
9	Fazal Kandahari	Kandahar	2		170		1	1	10						10	
10	Mirwais Nika	Kandahar	2		1500		1	1	15						15	
11	Aino No. 1	Kandahar		1		75	1	1	2						2	
12	Mahri Herawi	Herat		3		1720	2	1	48						48	
13	Jabraiel Girls Scho	Herat		2		300	1	1	20						20	
14	Istaclal	Balkh	2	1	2400					3					3	
15	Sitara	Balkh	3	1		550	1	2	2						2	
16	Sayed Hedayat Na	Balkh	2	1	800	162	1	2	10						2	
17	Kayanat Private	Kabul	2		245		1	1	10						10	
18	Makhfi Badakhshi	Kabul		3		1000	1	1	8						8	
19	Mariam	Kabul		4		1320	1		18						18	
20	Ghulam Mohamd	Kabul	1	2	700		1	1	14		1	1			14	
21	Rabia Balkhi	Kabul		2		2000	1	1	23			1	1	1	23	
22	Spin Kalai	Kabul		1		716	1	1								
23	Nahid Shahid	Kabul		1		1500	1	1		1		1				
24	Abo Zar Ghafari	Kabul		1	700		1	1				1		1	1	
25	Mahmood Tarzi	Kabul		1	1200											
26	Aliwozir	Kabul	1	1	470											
27	Ab. Ali Mostaghni	Kabul	1	1	1500		1	1	18						18	
28	Ghulam Haidar Kh	Kabul	1		3415		1	1	22						22	
29	Mahmood Hotaki	Kabul	1		900	1373	1	1	7						7	
30	Rokhshana	Kabul		1					17						17	
31	Ghazi	Kabul	2	1	2940		1	1	10			2			10	
32	Ghafoor Nadim	Kabul	2	2	2200		1	1	12			3			12	
33	Bibi Sarwari Sanga	Kabul		1		1600	1		18						18	
	Summary	17 Kabul / 5 Herat / 4 Nangarhar / 4 Kandahar / 3 Balkh	26	39	23940	13832	24	19	11	4	1	9	1	1	375	0

54

No	Name of School	Chair	Desk	Projector	Internet	Electricity Gov	Electricity Solar	Electricity Gen	Supported	Happy with Computer Education
1	Batti Koot	7	7		N	Y	N	N	Y	AV
2	Saifi Girls School	5	5		N	Y	N	Y	N	N
3	Amarkhail	8	8		N	N	N	Y	Y	N
4	Shahid Arif	11	11		N	Y	N	Y	Y	Y
5	Hawza Karbaz	10	10	1	Y	Y	N	Y	N	AV
6	Babashti				N	Y	N	Y	N	AV
7	Alayee	37	37	2	Y	Y	Y	Y	Y	Y
8	Ahmad Shah Baba	17	17		N	Y	N	Y	N	AV
9	Fazal Kandahari	10	10		N	Y	Y	Y	N	Y
10	Mirwais Nika	15	15		Y	Y	N	N	N	Y
11	Aino No.1	2	2		Y	N	N	N	N	N
12	Mahri Herawi	48	48	1	N	Y	N	Y	Y	Y
13	Jabraial Girls Scho	20	20		Y	Y	N	Y	Y	Y
14	Istaqlal	3	3		N	Y	N	N	N	AV
15	Sitara	2	2		N	Y	N	N	N	N
16	Sayed Hedayat Na	2	2		N	Y	Y	Y	N	AV
17	Kayanat Private	10	10	1	N	Y	N	N	N	Y
18	Makhfi Badakhshi	8	8	1	N	Y	N	N	N	Y
19	Mariam	18	18		Y	Y	N	N	N	AV
20	Ghulam Mohamed	25	14		Y	Y	N	N	N	Y
21	Rabia Balkhi	23	23	1	Y	Y	N	Y	N	Y
22	Spin Kalai				N	Y	N	Y	Y	Y
23	Nahid Shahid	1		1	N	Y	N	Y	N	N
24	Abo Zar Ghafari		1	1	N	Y	N	N	N	AV
25	Mahmood Tarzi				N	Y	N	N	N	AV
26	Alawdin				N	Y	N	N	N	N
27	Ab. Ali Mostaghni	50	50	1	N	Y	N	Y	Y	Y
28	Ghulam Haidar Kh	15	15	1	N	Y	N	N	N	N
29	Mahmood Hotaki	17	17	1	N	Y	N	N	N	Y
30	Rokhshana	17	4		N	Y	N	N	N	Y
31	Ghazi	10	4		N	Y	N	Y	N	Y
32	Ghafoor Nadim	24	12	1	N	Y	N	N	N	AV
33	Bibi Sarwari Sanga				N	Y	N	N	N	AV
	Summary	398	369	14	6 / 27	30 / 3	3 / 30	13 / 20	13 / 20	11 Average / 15 Yes / 7 No

55

Appendix II: Summary of Teacher's survey

Summary of Suvery about Computer Education with Computer Teacher of Schools in Afghanistan

No	Name	Province	Degree	Gender	Email	Proficiency	Field
1	Karishma Jan	Nangarhar	12th	Female	Y	N	
2	Ziba Jan	Nangarhar	12th	Female	Y	N	
3	Lila Herawai	Herat	14th	Female	N	N	
4	Fazela Jan Karimi	Herat	Bachelor	Female	N	N	
5	Aysha Jan	Herat	Bachelor	Female	N	N	
6	Jawed Jan	Nangarhar	Bachelor	Male	Y	Y	Database
7	Amrudin	Nangarhar	14th	Male	N	N	
8	Feroz Khan	Kandahar	Bachelor	Male	N	N	
9	Bashir Ahmad	Kandahar	Bachelor	Male	N	N	
10	Sayda Jan	Kandahar	Bachelor	Male	N	N	
11	Malalai Achakzai	Kandahar	12th	Female	N	N	
12	Momana	Herat	Bachelor	Female	Y	Y	General
13	Marzia	Herat	Bachelor	Female	Y	Y	General
14	Karima Jan	Herat	14th	Female	N	N	
15	Waheedullah	Balkh	14th	Male	N	N	
16	Fahim	Balkh	12th	Male	N	N	
17	Ramin	Balkh	14th	Male	N	N	
18	Wida Jan	Balkh	14th	Female	N	N	
19	Nadia	Balkh	12th	Female	N	N	
20	Fereshta Yaqobi	Kabul	Bachelor	Female	N	N	
21	Ahmad Farhad	Kabul	14th	Male	Y	Y	General
22	Hosai	Kabul	Bachelor	Female	N	N	
23	Balqis	Kabul	Bachelor	Female	Y	N	
24	Zuhra Tamana	Kabul	Bachelor	Female	N	N	
25	Salam Hussain	Kabul	14th	Male	Y	Y	General
26	Mahbooba Nasimi	Kabul	14th	Female	N	N	
27	Malalai Arifi	Kabul	Bachelor	Female	N	N	
28	Zarmina	Kabul	Bachelor	Female	N	N	
29	Malalai Ghairat	Kabul	Bachelor	Female	N	N	
30	Nasrin	Kabul	Bachelor	Female	N	N	
31	Malalai	Kabul	Bachelor	Female	N	N	
32	Masooda	Kabul	Bachelor	Female	Y	Y	General
33	Roya	Kabul	Bachelor	Female	N	N	
34	Sitara	Kabul	Bachelor	Female	N	N	
35	Sohila Nazami	Kabul	Bachelor	Female	Y	N	
36	Atifa	Kabul	Bachelor	Female	Y	N	
37	Nahida	Kabul	14th	Female	Y	N	
38	Zohal	Kabul	14th	Female	Y	Y	Database
39	Shakiba	Kabul	14th	Female	N	N	
40	Mohmd. Ismayel	Kabul	14th	Male	N	N	
41	Mohmd. Idriss	Kabul	Bachelor	Male	N	N	
42	Ajmal	Kabul	12th	Male	N	Y	General
43	Mohmd. Arif	Kabul	Bachelor	Male	Y	N	
44	Liloma	Kabul	Bachelor	Female	N	N	
45	Asadullah	Kabul	14th	Male	Y	Y	General
46	Zohra	Kabul	Bachelor	Female	Y	Y	General
47	Shafiqullah	Kabul	14th	Male	Y	Y	General
48	Hasina	Kabul	Bachelor	Female	Y	N	
Summary		29 Kabul 6 Herat 4 Nangarhar 4 Kandahar 5 Balkh	6 12th 15 14th 27 Bachelor	16 Male 32	18 Yes 30	11 Yes 37	9 General 2

56

Summary of Suvery about Computer Education with Computer Teacher of Schools in Afghanistan

No	Name	Devices used in teaching				Familiarity with Open Source	Open Source in Curriculum	Passing status of students	Future Chances of Students	Happy with Computer Education
		PC	Laptop	Projector	Others					
1	Karishma Jan	Y	Y	Y	N	N	N	Average	Y	Y
2	Ziba Jan	Y	N	Y	N	N	N	Good	Y	Y
3	Lila Herawai	N	N	N	N	N	N	Average	M	N
4	Fazela Jan Karimi	Y	Y	Y	N	N	N	Good	M	AV
5	Aysha Jan	Y	N	Y	N	N	N	Good	N	Y
6	Jawed Jan	Y	Y	Y	Y	Y	Y	Very Good	Y	Y
7	Amrudin	N	N	N	N	Y	Y	Average	Y	Y
8	Feroz Khan	Y	Y	N	N	Y	Y	Average	N	AV
9	Bashir Ahmad	Y	N	N	N	N	N	Average	Y	AV
10	Sayda Jan	Y	N	N	N	N	N	Average	M	Y
11	Malalai Achakzai	Y	N	N	N	N	N	Good	Y	Y
12	Momana	Y	N	Y	N	Y	Y	Good	Y	Y
13	Marzia	Y	N	Y	N	Y	Y	Good	Y	AV
14	Karima Jan	Y	N	N	N	N	N	Average	M	Y
15	Waheedullah	Y	N	N	N	N	N	Good	Y	N
16	Fahim	Y	N	N	N	N	N	Good	Y	N
17	Ramin	Y	N	N	N	Y	Y	Average	M	Y
18	Wida Jan	Y	N	N	N	N	N	Average	Y	Y
19	Nadia	N	Y	N	N	N	N	Good	M	Y
20	Fereshta Yaqobi							Good	Y	AV
21	Ahmad Farhad	Y	N	N	N	Y	N	Average	Y	Y
22	Hosai	Y	N	Y	N	N	N	Average	Y	Y
23	Balqis	Y	N	N	N	N	N	Very Good	Y	Y
24	Zuhra Tamana	Y	N	N	N	N	N	Average		N
25	Salam Hussain	Y	N	Y	N	Y	Y	Average	Y	Y
26	Mahbooba Nasimi	Y	N	Y	N	N	N	Average	N	Y
27	Malalai Arifi	N	Y	N	N	N	N	Average	N	Y
28	Zarmina	Y	N	Y	N	N	N	Good	Y	Y
29	Malalai Ghairat	Y	N	Y	N			Good		Y
30	Nasrin	Y	N	Y	N	N	N	Good	Y	Y
31	Malalai	Y	N	Y	N	N	N	Very Good	Y	N
32	Masooda	N	Y	Y	N	Y	Y	Average	Y	Y
33	Roya	Y	Y	N	N	N	N	Good	Y	AV
34	Sitara	Y	N	Y	N	N	N	Good	N	Y
35	Sohila Nazami	N	Y	N	N	N	N			Y
36	Atifa	Y	Y	Y	N	N	N	Average	Y	Y
37	Nahida	Y	Y	Y	Y	N	N	Good	Y	Y
38	Zohal	Y	Y	Y	Y	Y	N	Very Good	Y	Y
39	Shakiba	Y	N	Y	N	Y	Y	Average		Y
40	Mohmd. Ismayel	Y	N	N	N	N	N		N	Y
41	Mohmd. Idriss	N	N	N	N	N	N	Average	N	Y
42	Ajmal	Y	N	N	N	Y	N	Average	Y	Y
43	Mohmd. Arif	N	Y	N	N	N	N	Average	Y	N
44	Liloma					N	N	Average	N	
45	Asadullah	Y	N	N	N	Y	Y	Good	Y	AV
46	Zohra	Y	N	Y	N	Y		Good	Y	Y
47	Shafiqullah	Y	Y	Y	Y	Y	Y	Average	Y	Y
48	Hasina	N	N	N	N			Average	Y	N
	Summary	37	14	23	4	15	11	4 Very Good 18 Good	6 Maybe 30 Yes	7 Average 33 Yes
		9	32	23	42	30	33	24 Average	8 No	7 No

57

Appendix III: Summary of teachers' survey

Summary of teachers' survey about Computer Education for Afghan Schools

1. **What is your opinion about the Computer Education curriculum, and which aspects do you think should be modified or added to the curriculum?**
- This curriculum is better and will help the students for their daily activities.
- The level of current curriculum is higher than the literacy level of the students, while it focuses more on practical concepts but there is no facility available in most of the schools for practical work.
- The application which are reflected in the curriculum are out dated, the curriculum should reflect the latest version of the applications.
- The syllabus written for 10 and 11 grades are not well sorted, we recommend a step by step presenting of the concepts. The syllabus which developed in current curriculum don't contain well aspects, it should have aspects which are needed for the students daily life. It would be better to have each application for the whole grade instead to split it into several grades.
- Schools don't receive the books of curriculum on time so the students can't get the entire content well.
- The syllabus on current curriculum is well designed and the contents are based on the knowledge level of the students but there are no professional teachers to teach them.
- The curriculum should be reviewed and approved by professional experts of Computer Science. It should be reviewed in consideration to the needs and opportunities of Afghan society.
- The first part of the book reflect Internet usage, it would be nice to have theoretical concepts instead. Most of the parts in the syllabus are repeated, therefore for each grade separate syllabi should be written.

2. **Which problems do you experience during the realization of this curriculum?**
- The lack of professional teachers and physical facilities with current curriculum is the challenging issues. The practical parts of curriculum can't be implemented in the schools nowadays.
- The teachers whom are teaching Computer Education, are non-professional and don't have facilities such as their own computer to get prepare for the classes.
- The teachers are not trained with an international computer teaching methodology.
- The teaching hours dedicated for computer education are too limited per week we recommend to extend these hours.

3. **Do you have familiarity with Open Source Community? (If yes, what do you think of its role in education process?)**
- The integration of Open Source in Computer Education syllabus will affect the education process and we encourage the authorities to do so.
- As students need practical application, therefore I don't recommend integrating Open Source application to the curriculum.
- Information regarding Open Source in theoretical part of curriculum is recommended.

4. **Current Computer Education curriculum more focus on application based teaching then concept based, what do you think about this?**
- The application based curriculum will help the students to use computer for their daily activities, therefore we prefer application based curriculum.
- For sure application based curriculum is required for Computer Education, but we prefer mixture of both application based and concept based curriculum.
- As application presents more computer usage we prefer to have more application in curriculum, so that the students could benefit from that.

5. **How do you cope with Internet and electricity connections, during teaching?**
- There are several problems not only the Internet and electricity but we cope with problems by teaching using white board.
- We can use a redundant solution to solve the emergent problem.
- In coordination with school administration a solution can be discussed and implemented.
- To cope the problem UPS or Generators can be used.

6. **How do you observe the role of library in your teaching?**
- The library has its own effect on computer education but still computer education needs more practice then theory.
- We recommend supporting libraries at schools with computer education books.

7. **How can be the Computer Education process all over Afghanistan improved?**
- The Computer Education can be improved by hiring professional teachers, developing a standard syllabus and providing teaching materials as physical facilities for schools.
- Beside other aspects improving schools administration will help the education process.
- The curriculum should be developed based on necessity of the society and its practical opportunities.
- The Computer Education teachers must be trained in order to provide better teaching.
- The authorities most work hard for improving computer education.
- The computer education don't have its importance to the officials, therefore they should know the importance of technology and computer education in schools.
- The peace and security is an important factor for development.

- The ministry of finance must allocate special budget for Computer Education to the ministry of education.
- A variety of experts should be trained in the field.
- For improving computer education all over Afghanistan it is necessary to have computer education started from preliminary schools.
- During the vacation it would be nice to held external courses for the students and training for the computer teachers.
- The current curriculum in not standard it should be revised.
- The families should support government for providing physical facilities and their children to grasp further knowledge of computer.
- Public awareness program should be deployed in order to encourage students and society to grasp their attention to this field.

Note: This is a complete summary of 48 questioners which were filled by school teachers. Only few of the survey participants replied to the question in English, the rest are translated from Pashto and Dari in this summary. This summary will be used to quote in my thesis; however the original questioner will be kept if there is any query about them.

Regards,
Sayed Abdullah Walizai
Master Student of Technical Univesity of Berlin
25-March-2013

Appendix IV: Summary of Ministry of Education staff's survey

Summary of Ministry of Education staff survey about computer education

1. **Could you please explain the planning for Computer Education?**
- Compiling new text books and teacher guides for those books.
- Distribute the published books to schools across Afghanistan.
- Provide computer and build labs in schools for computer education.

2. **How is the current status of Computer Education in Afghan Schools?**
- The syllabus (textbook) for computer education for students are compiled and already published.
- A teacher guide to each textbook for computer education is under working.
- Lack of physical facilities is a big problem with our current syllabus.

3. **The current syllabus of Computer Education for high school is more application based, and then concept based, what is your idea about the new syllabus?**
- The syllabus will be reviewed and will be newly published in 1393 (same to 2014) and based on research we will include further concepts and ideas.
- Computer Science related concepts can be added later in university curriculum, but for schools it is necessary to focus on application based approaches.

4. **The current syllabi more present Computer Usage then Computer Science, how is the plan to focus more on Computer Science then its usage?**
- Due to necessity of society the computer usage is the main part of syllabus, for the future we will focus more on concepts.

5. **How is the overall policy of Ministry about Open Source Community and how it will be integrated in Computer Education?**
- Open Source is very good for our situation. We will introduce this in a chapter in our new syllabus.

6. **What is the policy of Ministry for Physical opportunities of Computer Education (e.g Labs, hardware etc.)?**

7. **As some schools are supported by individual organization or PRT teams, they have some Computer Facilities, while other schools don't have such facilities. As policy of Ministry of Education is to present unique education for all citizens, so how this will be balanced in future that all schools will have Computer Education facilities?**

8. **How is the importance of Computer Education to Ministry policy makers then other subjects?**

9. **What do you think of one-laptop-per-child project and how is its current status?**

10. **What is the policy of Ministry for covering provinces in Computer Education?**

11. **It is very ideal that all schools across Afghanistan will have Internet access, in the meanwhile the current syllabi focus on Internet application usage. How is this reflected to students?**
12. **Although some institutions are providing vocational trainings for Computer Education teachers, what is the specific plan for training teachers for Computer Educations in Ministry of Education?**
- A book as teacher guide will be published soon which will help the teachers to teach professionally.
13. **Society doesn't have enough knowledge of Computer Science, what is the plan of Ministry in providing public awareness for the people?**
14. **How will be information and communication technology (ICT) integrated in other subject of schools?**
- We have some lesson in other subject about ICT. Like history, languages and in civic education.
15. **Is there any specific board which works on Computer Education? If yes a little information about that.**

Note: This is a complete summary of 3 questioners which were filled by Ministry of Education staff. This summary will be used to quote in my thesis; however the original questioner will be kept if there is any query about them.

Regards,
Sayed Abdullah Walizai
Master Student of Technical Univesity of Berlin
08-April-2013

Appendix V: Summary of Afghan Computer Science Professionals Survey

Summary of Computer Science Professionals Survey about Computer Education in Schools

8. **What is your opinion about the Computer Education curriculum, and which aspects do you think should be modified or added to the curriculum?**
- There should be a computer literacy course starting in 7th class up to 12th class through which basic knowledge of computer literacy can be taught.
- The current curriculum is not well, coz it is for high school only; instead it should cover all levels of school.
- The curriculum should be based on the need of society.

9. **Which problems do you experience during the realization of this curriculum?**
- Lack or shortage of Lab equipment and exceed number of students in one class. The curriculum don't have infrastructure for practical work.
- It should fulfill international standards.
- This curriculum is good but there are some environmental factors which cause problems in the applicability of the curriculum.
- Not enough number of computer teachers to teach computer education to the students in the schools.

10. **What do you think of Open Source Community integration in curriculums?**
- It is a good idea. Since our country is economically struggling, we have to migrate from close source to open source.
- The main problem with Open Source Software is the lack of familiarity with that. The publics don't know how to use Open Source.
- As Open Source is growing all over the world, therefore it should be included in school curriculum.
- For students in Open Source there are several resources that can help them.
- The preliminary education of the computer in the education sector of Afghanistan should be strengthened first then Open Source can be integrated.

11. **Current Computer Education curriculum more focus on application based teaching then concept based, what do you think about this?**
- As there are fewer infrastructures, therefore the chance of practical work is less in schools so it is good to consider concepts in curriculum.

- To populate concept based computer education in the education system of Afghanistan, we need large number of people who have knowledge of concept based computer education.

12. How relevant is current computer education courses to the future chances of the students (i.e. how well it fits the needs of the situation in Afghanistan).

- The current curriculum is too weak and cannot fulfill the needs of society.
- The school curriculum should be developed in close coordination of computer science departments and faculties in universities to be more effective.
- The current platform of the computer education in Afghanistan is going through its first phases and the products of this computer education system will be analyzed after seeing the impact of education on these students after the graduation from 12th. Nevertheless, this system is having a positive impact on the careers of the people but improvements and positive changes will lead this system to be more effective.

13. How can be the Computer Education process all over Afghanistan improved?

- It needs a proper curriculum.
- It requires governmental supports.
- The computer teachers should be trained.
- For standard education infrastructure is the important factor.
- The current curriculum should be revised by computer science experts.
- Computer Education strategy should be developed by MoE and MoHE.
- Security has direct impact on the education system of Afghanistan if our country is led to peace and prosperity; we will witness a lot of effective changes, with the current state of the country, we may not expect all the education centers of Afghanistan for the effective computer education especially far sighted districts and villages. In Afghanistan still more than 80% of schools don't have electricity and other critical things for making an effective environment for education, to improve the computer education in the country, we need to work on enhancing computer education on school level, by creating computer education centers in each district and providing all the facilities for those computer education centers.

14. The current syllabi more present Computer Usage then Computer Science, what is your idea to focus more on Computer Science then its usage?

- As computer science is a new filed in Afghanistan, therefore it is necessary to reflect information about that in school curriculum.
- It is very important to focus more on the Conceptual education and the importance of computer science, the students should be given trainings on, how

computers have been created, and how computer works and how to use computer better.

15. **How can be information and communication technology (ICT) integrated in other subject of schools?**
- The curriculum for school must provide a base for university studies and it should be implementable in all provinces.
- The first focus should be on computer education and afterward ICT integration can be taken into consideration.
- Giving information on the importance of ICT in the real life, students must have ability to use Internet, use ICT for communication, efficiency, showing them the usage of ICT for all their subjects. The involvement of ICT in all the subjects, books and teaching materials are not up to date and not according to market, here technology can play vital role

16. **Society doesn't have enough knowledge of Computer Science, what is your idea for providing public awareness for the people?**
- The government must support computer science.
- The application Software should be localized to local languages.
- In school curriculum computer studies should be integrated.
- Improve the computer literacy among the students and employees.
- Trainings on provincial, district and village level, workshops, conferences, showing benefits of using computerized system compared to the manual system, showing the positive impact of computer science in the financial and economical , educational and infrastructure growth of the country.

Note: This is a complete summary of 7 questioners which were filled by computer science professionals in different universities of Afghanistan. This summary will be used to quote in my thesis; however the original questioner will be kept if there is any query about them.

Regards,
Sayed Abdullah Walizai
Master Student of Technical Univesity of Berlin
02-April-2013

Printed by Books on Demand GmbH, Norderstedt / Germany